What All Good Dogs Should Know

What All Good Dogs Should Know

THE SENSIBLE WAY TO TRAIN

Jack Volhard
and Melissa Bartlett

Hungry Minds, Inc.

Hungry Minds, Inc.
909 Third Avenue
New York, NY 10022

Library of Congress Cataloging-in-Publication Data
Volhard, Joachim.
    What all good dogs should know: the sensible way to train/Jack Volhard and Melissa Bartlett.
        p. cm.
    Includes bibliographical references.
    ISBN 0-87605-832-2
    1. Dogs—Training. 2. Dogs—Behavior. I. Bartlett, Melissa.
II. Title.
SF431.V65 1991
636.7'088'7—dc20   90-46718   CIP

30 29 28 27 26 25 24 23 22 21

Printed in the United States of America

To our teachers:

Canem familiaris

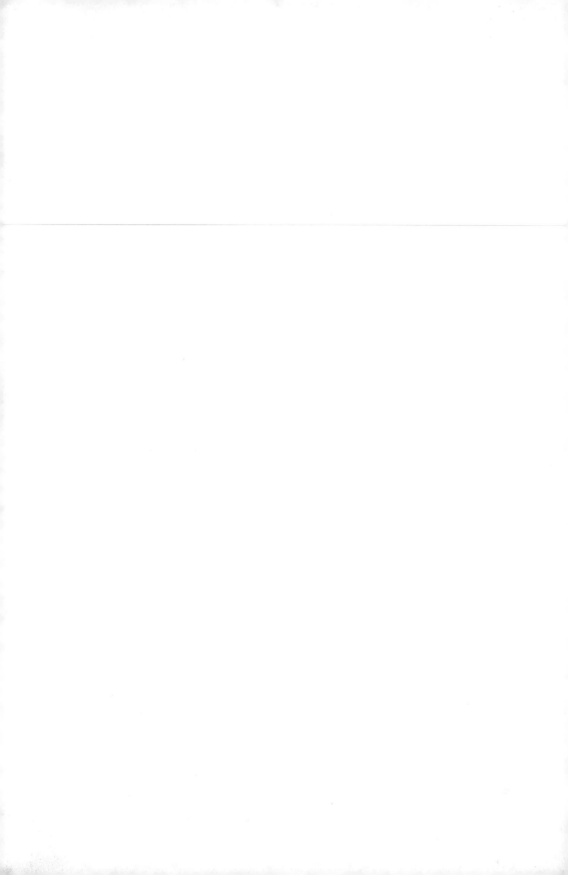

Contents

About the Authors

Jack Volhard, internationally known as a "trainer of trainers," is the recipient of five awards from the Dog Writers' Association of America (DWAA), senior author of *Training Your Dog: The Step-by-Step Manual* (Howell Book House, 1983), named Best Care and Training Book for 1983 by the DWAA; *Teaching Dog Obedience Classes: The Manual for Instructors* (Howell Book House, 1986), acclaimed as "the state-of-the-art text for instructors"; the videotapes "Puppy Aptitude Testing," named Best Film on Dogs for 1980 by the DWAA, "Teaching Dog Obedience Classes: Level 1" (1988), "Open Training: The Teaching Phase" (1990) and "Utility Training: The Teaching Phase" (1990). He has also authored more than a hundred articles for various dog publications.

Over the past twenty years, through his obedience classes, lectures, seminars and training camps, he has taught more than ten thousand people how to communicate with their dogs, how to make training fun for both owner and dog and thereby achieve a mutually rewarding relationship.

Melissa Bartlett, named Dog Cartoonist of the Year for 1987 by the Dog Writers' Association of America, had her first article, "A Novice Looks at Puppy Aptitude Testing," published by the *American Kennel*

Gazette in 1979. Since then her numerous articles and delightful illustrations have appeared in various publications, and she was the illustrator for *Training Your Dog: The Step-by-Step Manual* and *Teaching Dog Obedience Classes: The Manual for Instructors.*

Fifteen years ago she started her training career in a class taught by Jack Volhard and since then has become involved in a variety of teaching activities, including helping handicapped people with their pets.

What All Good Dogs Should Know

1

Why Train
Your Dog?

TRAINED DOGS ARE "FREE" DOGS. They are welcome almost anywhere because they behave around people and other dogs, because they stay when told and come when called. They are a pleasure to take for a walk and can be let loose for a romp in the park. They can be taken on trips and family outings. They are members of the family in every sense of the word.

Untrained dogs have few, if any, privileges. When guests come, they are locked away because they are too unruly. When the family sits down to eat, they are locked up or put outside because of begging at the table. If allowed off leash, they run away and stay out for hours at a time. Nobody wants to walk them because they pull, and family outings with such a nuisance are forbidden.

Your dog has a life expectancy of eight to sixteen years. Now is the time to ensure these years are going to be mutually rewarding. Teach your dog what all *good* dogs should know.

WHAT IS A GOOD DOG?

Dog books tell us that all breeds are loyal, obedient, trustworthy, good with children, born protectors and wonderful companions. Dogs

A trained dog is a member of the family.

have the potential to be great pets, but few come that way. Most require some training to bring out the best in them and to help them live up to these expectations.

A good dog must:

1. be housetrained
2. come when called
3. have no bad habits
4. stay when told
5. not pull when taken for a walk.

Number 3 includes not biting the hand that feeds you, or any other friendly soul, no excessive barking, no destructive chewing and, of course, no jumping up on anyone unless specifically invited.

Depending on your dog, and what you expect, the dog may need training in just a few of these areas or in all five.

WHAT IS INVOLVED IN TRAINING?

It may come as a surprise to you, but your dog's ancestors were bred for the ability to do a particular job well. Looks were considered

Most dogs require some training to become perfect pets.

incidental. How readily you can train your dog to fit into your life-style will depend on the job for which it was bred. For example, it will be easier to train a dog bred to guard to stay on the property than a dog bred to hunt.

Today, most owners—and we suspect you did, too—chose their pets on appearance—"what a cute puppy!" When you selected your puppy, did you consider how instincts for which it was selectively bred over countless generations affect behavior as an adult?

Fortunately, some of these instincts are the very ones that endear the dog to us and make it such a good pet, such as the legendary protecting of children, the warning bark when a stranger comes on the property, the friendly greeting when you come home and the comfort provided in times of sorrow. Characteristics of specific breeds, such as the Newfoundland's rescue instincts, the Bernese Mountain Dog's willingness to pull a cart, a Terrier's untiring playfulness, and the Labrador's eagerness to retrieve, are just as endearing.

Other instincts get the dog into trouble. A dog bred for guarding

Newfoundlands were bred for rescue.

that does the job too well is accused of being vicious; one bred for herding is chastised for chasing children, joggers, bicycles and cars; and the hunting dog is punished for following a scent. Only the lap dog can get away with almost anything.

Other instincts get the dog into trouble.

From cute puppy to adult.

For Barbara and Ed it was love at first sight with Bentley the Mastiff puppy. On impulse, they brought Bentley home from the pet store. When he grew into a huge dog and took to knocking down the postman, they were horrified. "He was such a cuddly puppy," they recalled, "just like a teddy bear." They did not realize that Bentley was just doing his job—Mastiffs were bred in England to guard estates. With a little training plus keeping a eye on Bentley when the postman was expected, the problem was resolved.

If what you are trying to teach your dog is in harmony with its instincts, training will be easy; if it goes against the dog's instincts, training will be more difficult. For example, it will be easier to teach a Labrador to retrieve than to teach a herding dog not to chase joggers.

It is easy to teach a Lab to fetch.

BUILDING TRUST

Picture your dog chasing a cat across the road. Your heart is in your mouth because you are afraid the dog might get run over. When Homer finally returns, you are angry and soundly scold him for chasing the cat and giving you such a scare.

Here is how *your dog* looks at this situation. First, he chased the cat, which was lots of fun. Then he came back to you and was reprimanded, which was no fun at all.

What you *wanted* to teach was not to chase the cat. What you *actually* taught was that coming to you can be unpleasant.

Lesson: Whether you are pleased or angry, your dog associates these feelings only with what was done *last*.

One of the commands you will want your dog to learn is to come when called. To be successful, remember this principle: *Whenever your dog comes to you, be nice.* Reward this behavior.

No matter what your dog may have done, be pleasant and use a kind word, a pat on the head and a smile. Teach your dog to trust you by being a safe place for him. When your dog is with you, follows you or comes to you, make the dog feel wanted.

When you call a dog to you and then punish, you undermine trust in you. When your dog comes to you voluntarily and gets punished, the dog associates being punished with coming to you.

You may ask, "How can I be nice when my dog brings me the remains of one of my brand-new shoes or wants to jump on me with muddy paws or when I just discovered an unwanted present on the carpet?" For the answers, you will have to read this book; it will show you how to deal with all these situations without undermining the dog's trust in you.

When Homer comes to you, make him feel wanted.

CONSISTENCY

If there is any magic to training, it is *consistency*. Your dog cannot understand "sometimes, maybe, perhaps or only on Sundays." Your dog *can* and does understand yes and no.

For example, it confuses your dog when you encourage jumping up on you when you are wearing old clothes, but then become angry when he joyfully plants muddy paws on your best suit.

Tom loved to wrestle with Tyson, his Boxer. Then one day, when Grandma came to visit, Tyson flattened her. Tom was angry and Tyson was confused—he thought roughhousing was a wonderful way to show affection. After all, that's what Tom had taught him.

Does this mean you can never permit your puppy to jump up on you? Not at all, but you have to train your pup that this is permitted *only* when you say it's OK. But beware: It is more difficult to train a dog to make this distinction than to train one not to jump up at all. The more "black and white" or "yes and no" you can make it, the easier it will be for your dog to understand what you want.

PERSISTENCE

Training your dog is a question of who is more persistent—you or your dog. Some things will be learned quickly; others will take more time. If several tries don't bring success, be patient, remain calm and

It's not a good idea to teach your dog to roughhouse.

try again. It sometimes takes many repetitions before a dog understands a command and responds to it each and every time.

TAKING CHARGE

It's not a matter of choice. Since dogs are pack animals, you and your family are now the pack. As far as your dog is concerned, no pack can exist without a leader, and it's either you or the dog. That's the way it *has* to be.

You must be pack leader.

For safety, *you* have to be in charge!

You may think that you really just want to be friends, partners or peers with your dog. You can be all of those, but for the well-being of your dog you must be the one in charge. In today's complicated world you cannot rely on your pet to make the decisions.

Denise did not think much about the being-in-charge theory. After all, Bruno, her Doberman, had never given her any trouble. She changed her mind when Bruno made the decision "now I will chase the cat across the road" just as a car was coming. She realized that if she wanted Bruno to be around for a while, he had to learn that *she* made the decisions.

Few dogs actively seek leadership, and most are perfectly content when you assume the role, as long as you do. But you *must* do so, or even the meekest of dogs will take over. Remember, it's not a matter of choice. For everyone's safety, you have to be the one in charge.

SIGNS TO WATCH

Does your dog take over your favorite armchair, constantly demanding attention? Are you ignored when you want the dog to move? Does your pet shoot out of doors ahead of you? If so, your dog is in charge and not you.

Without leadership, even the meekest dog will take over.

Part of a dog's behavior may be due to a lack of education, and the first order of business is to begin training. Start with teaching the dog to sit on command (chapter 7) and to lie down on command (chapter 8). Both of these exercises not only help you to control your dog, an important part of dog ownership, but they also teach the dog that *you* are in charge.

After you have trained your dog, use what you have taught on a regular basis. For example:

1. make him sit before you give food or *any* treat
2. make him sit before you pet him
3. make him sit and stay before you go through a door.

Toshiba, Richard's Akita, constantly crashed through doors ahead of her owner, ignored commands and growled when Richard wanted her off the sofa. Richard realized he had to train Toshiba and he did.

He trained her to sit and behave before she was petted or got any treats, and to stay off the furniture and lie on the rug instead. What most impressed Richard was the change in Toshiba's attitude: She seemed calmer, more relaxed and happier. "I guess she really wanted me to be in charge all along," Richard commented.

11

Make your dog sit before you give a treat.

Begin the training as soon as possible after you have obtained your dog. Then use it consistently to make it clear that you are in charge. You now have a trained dog that looks to you for leadership and that is a real joy to have around.

SUMMARY

1. A trained dog is a free dog.
2. How readily you can train your dog to fit your life-style will depend on the task for which the dog was bred.
3. Whenever your dog comes to you, be nice. Reward this.
4. If there is any magic to training, it is consistency.
5. As far as your dog is concerned, no pack can exist without a leader, and it's either you or your dog.
6. For safety, you have to be the one in charge.

2

What Happens When

FROM BIRTH UNTIL MATURITY, your dog goes through physical and mental developmental periods. These, in turn, affect the dog's behavior.

THE FORTY-NINTH DAY AND BONDING

The age at which a puppy is separated from its mother and littermates influences behaviors important to becoming a good pet. At about the forty-ninth day of life, when the puppy is neurologically complete, that special attachment between dog and owners, called *bonding,* starts. For this reason, this is the ideal time for the puppy to leave the nest for its new home.

A puppy separated from its canine family before that day, say at the thirty-fifth day (fifth week), may develop an unhealthy attachment to humans. Typical behaviors are overprotectiveness of the owner and aggression toward other dogs, nervousness and excessive barking.

From the thirty-fifth day on, the mother also teaches her puppies basic doggie manners. She communicates to the puppies what is unacceptable behavior and, if necessary, growls, snarls or snaps at them as a form of discipline. For example, during weaning she teaches the puppies to leave her alone. After just a few repetitions, the puppies begin to respond to a mere look from her or a curled lip.

Puppy/human bonding continuum.

A puppy that has not had these important lessons may find it difficult to accept discipline as it grows up.

A puppy left with its mother or littermates for much longer than the seventh week will grow up being too dog-oriented. Bonding to humans will tend to be difficult, if possible at all, as will be teaching the dog to accept responsibility for its own behavior. The dog will not care about its human family and will be hard to train.

Tessa lived in a large kennel with some of her littermates and other dogs. She received little human attention. When she was seven months old, Carol bought her as a pet. Carol quickly discovered that Tessa was fearful of new situations, was terrified of car rides and distrusted people.

Tessa had stayed with other dogs too long and now was only comfortable in a kennel setting around other dogs.

THE NEED TO SOCIALIZE
(weeks seven through twelve)

Your dog is a social animal. To become an acceptable pet, the pup needs to interact with you, your family and other humans and dogs during the seventh through the twelfth weeks of life. Denied that, your dog's behavior around other people or dogs may be unpredictable— either fearful or aggressive. For example, unless regularly meeting children during this period, a dog may not be trustworthy around them, especially when feeling cornered.

Your puppy needs the chance to meet and to have positive experiences with those beings that will play a role in its life. If you are a grandparent whose grandchildren occasionally visit, have your puppy meet children as often as you can. If you live by yourself but have

Socialize your puppy.

friends visit you, make an effort to let your puppy meet other people, particularly members of the opposite sex. If you plan on taking your puppy to obedience class or dog shows or ultimately using the dog in a breeding program, you should both be interacting with other dogs.

If you plan to take your dog on family outings or vacations, introduce riding in a car. Time spent *now* is well worth the effort in making your puppy the well-adjusted companion you want in a grown dog.

Encourage your puppy to follow you.

This is also a time when your puppy will follow your every footstep. Encourage this behavior by rewarding with an occasional treat, a pat on the head or a kind word.

FEAR PERIOD
(weeks eight through twelve)

Avoid exposing the puppy to traumatic experiences during this period because they may have a lasting impact. For example, elective surgery, such as ear cropping, should be done before eight or after eleven weeks of age. When you take the puppy to the veterinarian have the doctor give the puppy a treat before, during and after the examination to make it a pleasant visit. A particularly stressful or unpleasant experience now can literally ruin a puppy for life.

During the first year's growth you may see fear reactions at other times. When you do, under no circumstances drag your puppy up to the object that caused the fear. Don't pet or reassure the dog—you may give the impression that you approve of this behavior. Rather, distract the puppy and go on to something pleasant. After a short time, the fearful behavior will disappear.

LEAVING HOME
(four to eight months)

Sometime between the fourth and eighth months, your puppy will begin to realize there is a big, wide world out there. Up to now, every time you have called, the pup willingly came to you. But now, your dog may want to investigate, perhaps even chase a cat or follow a trail. The dog is maturing and cutting the apron strings. This is normal. Your puppy is not being spiteful or disobedient, just becoming an adolescent.

While going through this phase, it is best to keep the pup on leash or in a confined area until your pet has learned to come when called. Otherwise, not coming when called will become an annoying and dangerous habit. Once this becomes the behavior, it will be difficult to change; prevention is the best cure. It is much easier to teach your dog to come when called *before* developing the habit of running away than afterwards. Chapter 10 teaches you how to train your dog to come when called.

16

Cutting the apron strings.

Under *no* circumstances play the game of chasing the dog. Instead, run the other way and try to get the dog to chase *you*. If that does not work, kneel on the ground and pretend you have found something extremely interesting, hoping your dog's curiosity will bring the animal to you. If you have to go to the dog, approach slowly until you can calmly hold the collar.

During this time your dog also goes through teething and needs to chew—anything and everything. Dogs, like children, can't help it. Your job is to provide acceptable outlets for this need, such as chew bones and toys. If one of your favorite shoes is demolished—puppies have the irritating habit of tackling many shoes (but only one from each pair)—try to control yourself. Look at it as a lesson to keep your possessions out of reach. Scolding will not stop the need to chew, but it *may* cause your pup to fear you.

GROWING UP
(one to four years)

No matter how much we might wish that cute little puppy to remain, it is going to grow up.

Maturity rates vary from breed to breed. Generally, the larger the dog, the longer it takes to become an adult. It happens anywhere from one to four years. During that time, a dog will undergo physical and

During teething give your dog suitable toys.

emotional changes. For you, as the owner, the most important one is the dog's sense of identity. To put it in a nutshell, every so often your puppy may push for a promotion, trying to be the one in charge, telling *you* what to do instead of the other way around. Again, this is perfectly normal, and all it requires is training the dog to understand who is the boss. Practicing the lessons contained in this book will put you on top.

Training will put you in charge.

WHEN TO START TRAINING

As soon as you bring your dog or puppy home, start training. Be consistent so that the dog learns only what you want it to know. Your puppy will learn, whether or not you train it. To prevent it from learning something you don't want, start training *now!*

SUMMARY

1. The ideal time for bonding is around the forty-ninth day.
2. Your dog is a social animal.
3. During the fear period, unpleasant experiences should be avoided.
4. It is easy to teach a dog to come when called *before* it has learned to run away.
5. In the development of a sense of identity, your dog may try to be the one in charge.
6. Start training your dog *now*.

Yes, dogs can think. The problem is that they think like dogs.

3

How Your
Dog Thinks

BEFORE LEAVING FOR WORK, Marcia always put Bella in her crate. It wasn't long before Bella went into her crate on her own when Marcia was about to leave. "What a clever puppy," thought Marcia. "She knows I am going to work."

CAN YOUR DOG READ YOUR MIND?

Dogs often give the appearance of being able to read our minds. What happens in actuality is that by observing us and studying our habits, they learn to anticipate our actions. Since they communicate with each other through body language, they quickly become experts at reading ours.

What Bella observed was that immediately before leaving for work, Marcia put on makeup and then crated her. Bella's cue to go into her crate was Marcia's putting on her makeup.

Then one evening, before dinner guests were to arrive, Marcia started putting makeup on. When Bella immediately went into her crate, Marcia realized the dog had not been reading her mind but had learned her routine through observation.

"READING" YOUR DOG

Just as your dog takes cues from watching you, so can *you* learn to interpret what's on your dog's mind by watching her.

You know Sasha has the habit of jumping up on the counter to see whether there is any food she can steal. Since she has done this a number of times before, you begin to recognize her intentions by the look on her face—head and ears are up, whiskers pointed forward, intent stare—and the way she moves in the direction of the counter—deliberately with her tail wagging.

It is at that point that you *interrupt* Sasha's naughty thoughts, *distract* her and give her a *command*.

Interrupt!

In a stern voice say "stop," or "ah, ah," whistle or sharply clap your hands or, as a last resort, blow a boat horn, which will make any dog stop in its tracks.

Distract!

Once you have interrupted her thoughts, distract her with a ball or a treat and call her to you. Reward her for coming by petting or giving a treat.

Command!

Then tell her to lie down. (See chapter 8.)

The next best choice is to catch her in the act and deal with her before she has completed whatever she is doing.

If you catch Sasha in the act of trying to steal food—she has her paws planted on the counter—firmly tell her to stop and physically remove her from the counter by her collar, take her to her corner and tell her to lie down.

Do not attempt any discipline *after* the offending deed has been done. Your dog cannot make the connection between the discipline and the offending deed. Your dog may look guilty, but not because she understands what she has done; she looks guilty because she understands you are upset.

Visualize yourself preparing a piece of meat for dinner. You leave the counter to answer the phone and after you return, the meat is

Interrupt.

Distract.

Command.

gone. You know Sasha ate it. Your first reaction is anger. Immediately Sasha looks guilty and you *assume* she knows she has done wrong.

Sasha knows no such thing. She is reacting to your anger and, perhaps based on prior experience, expects to be the target of your wrath.

Look at it from Sasha's point of view. The meat is gone and she thoroughly enjoyed it. You can't bring it back or make her un-enjoy it. What's worse, if you punish Sasha now, she will not even understand why, because she can't make the connection between the punishment

Second choice—catch your dog in the act.

and the meat she just ate. She can only make the connection between your anger and being punished.

She knows you are angry but does not know it has anything to do with the meat.

Moral of story: Don't leave meat unattended on the counter.

We do not recommend use of the word "no." Just yelling "no" at the poor dog for everything and anything will only confuse her and make her neurotic. Instead, be specific. If you don't want her to jump on you, tell her to sit. If you don't want her on the couch, teach her the word "off," and so on.

If you attribute human qualities and reasoning abilities to your dog, your dealings are doomed to failure. Your pet certainly does not experience guilt. Blaming the dog because "he ought to know better" or "she shouldn't have done it," or exclaiming "how could she do this to me?" will not improve behavior. Your pet also does not "understand every word you say," and is only able to interpret your tone of voice.

Do not attempt any discipline after the fact.

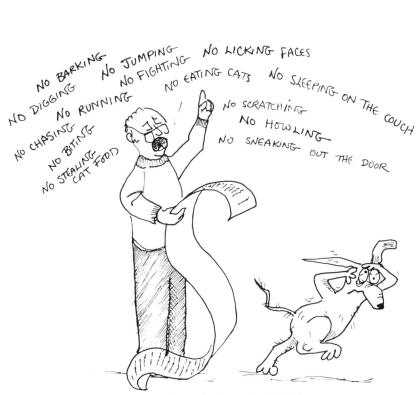

Instead of "no," give a command.

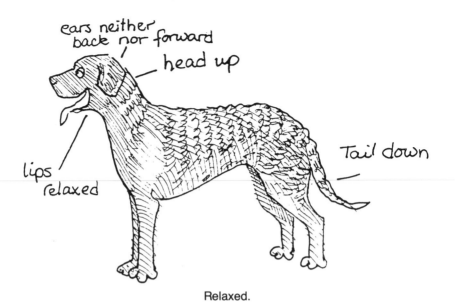

Relaxed.

BODY STANCES

Following are six body stances that will help you interpret what's on your dog's mind.

Relaxed

A relaxed dog is calm and ready to be trained. It will be easy to get the attention focused on you.

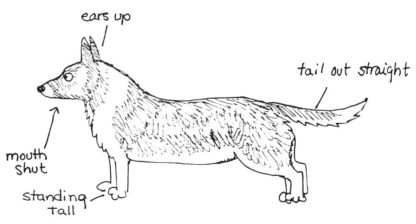

Alert.

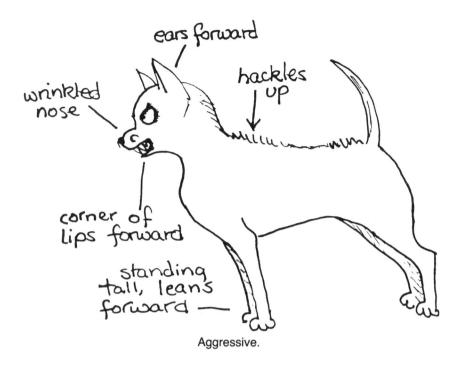

ears forward

hackles up

wrinkled nose

corner of lips forward

standing tall, leans forward —

Aggressive.

Alert

The dog has sensed something. It could be the family car approaching, a cat, another dog or the mail carrier. What comes next depends on your dog's temperament. For example, if it is a cat, Fido may give chase. *Now* is the right time to tell him to stop.

Aggressive

This position warns that the dog may bite. Definitely *interrupt, distract* and *command*.

Appeasing

This signals "I want to be friends." Princess is pleased to be in the presence of someone she considers superior. She is not feeling guilty, but is doing everything possible to let you know she is going along with whatever you say. If this is a puppy, she may urinate. Do not discipline for urinating because it will not make her stop, but make it worse.

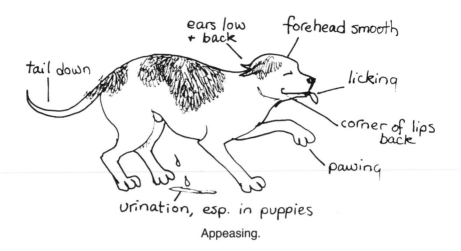

ears low + back

forehead smooth

tail down

licking

corner of lips back

pawing

urination, esp. in puppies

Appeasing.

Submissive

This posture says "I give up. Don't hurt me. You've won." *Distract* and do something pleasant for the dog.

Stressed

This dog is overloaded. Whatever the situation, it is too much for this dog. *Distract* and do something pleasant for the dog.

The more time you spend observing your dog, the better you get at interpreting what's on Kato's mind. Your dog is already an expert and you can become one, too.

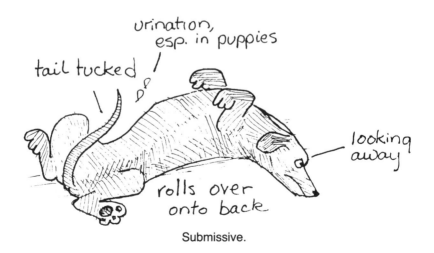

urination, esp. in puppies

tail tucked

looking away

rolls over onto back

Submissive.

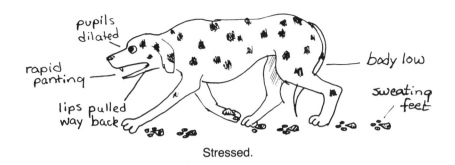

pupils dilated

rapid panting

lips pulled way back

body low

sweating feet

Stressed.

Learn to "read" your dog.

SUMMARY

1. Dogs are experts at reading body language.
2. The best time to stop undesirable behavior is when your dog is thinking about it.
3. Discipline after the offending deed is ineffective.
4. Your dog does not understand the concept of guilt.
5. Your dog does not understand every word you say.
6. By observing, you can learn to read your dog's mind.

4

Who Is Training Whom?

TRAINING QUIZ

What do you do when your dog:

1. drops a ball in your lap while you are watching television?
2. nudges or paws your elbow when you are sitting on the couch?
3. rattles the food dish?
4. sits at the door?

If your answers are:

1. throw it
2. pet the dog
3. fill the dish
4. open the door

your dog has you well trained!

Training is a two-way street. Laddie is just as much involved in training you as you are in training him.

Your dog has trained you well.

YOUR DOG

Your dog learns through daily experiences, some of which are pleasant, some not.

For example, Laddie the Collie, while pawing at the gate one day, accidentally opened it and took himself for a nice long walk in the neighborhood. From then on, whenever he wanted to go for a walk, he would paw at the gate until it opened.

Max, the Dachshund, did not fare as well. One winter day he was walking near the garage when a huge pile of snow slid off the roof and buried him. He now makes a big arc around the garage.

Experiences that are neutral for the dog don't make much of an impression and are quickly forgotten. For the dog to remember the event or situation, it has to be memorable, either good or bad from its point of view.

A behavior that is no longer rewarded is soon forgotten. For example, Heidi had cleverly learned how to open the cupboard in which the dog biscuits were kept and freely helped herself. Her owner, alarmed at the increase in Heidi's waistline, put a lock on the door.

Laddie learned to open the gate.

Max remembers being buried by snow.

After a while, Heidi stopped trying to open the cupboard.

Since Heidi's efforts were no longer successful, she soon stopped trying to open the cupboard door.

YOU AND YOUR DOG

Every time you interact with your dog some form of training takes place. You may not be aware of it at the time, but it will shape behavior.

For example, when Deacon was a puppy, nobody thought anything about slipping him something from the dinner table. Now he is six months old—almost fully grown—and he begs at the table.

What happened? He was trained to beg by being given food from the table. Since it is no longer cute, everyone wants to put a stop to it. The family resolves not to feed him from the table anymore. At first,

You are responsible for shaping behavior.

Deacon does not believe this is happening and he digs a little deeper into his repertoire of begging routines. Sure enough, someone takes pity on him and slips him a treat.

As this scenario repeats itself, often with longer intervals before someone gives in, Deacon is systematically being trained *do not to take "no" for an answer* or *persistence pays!*

Looking at it from Deacon's point of view, you are rewarding and encouraging the very behavior you find objectionable.

As soon as you stop giving in to Deacon, his efforts will decrease, until over time and *provided* you don't have a relapse, he will stop begging altogether. In technical jargon, you have extinguished the undesired behavior by refusing to reward it.

Good training rewards the desired behavior and discourages or ignores the undesired behavior. Start *good* training by paying attention to what you are rewarding and ask yourself: *Do I really want my*

Do not give in!

dog to do this? Is this something I want to live with as long as I have this dog? If the answers are no, then *stop* rewarding these behaviors.

What about this situation? Fifi just had a good chase after another dog. Your heart was in your mouth because you were afraid she would get run over; you call her and she comes rushing back to you. Which behavior do you want to reward/which discourage?

Easy, you say. I want to discourage chasing and reward coming when called. Excellent, and how are you going to do that?

In this example, you can do *nothing* about Fifi having chased another dog. You can *only* reward the coming when called. It is the *last* behavior Fifi remembers. If you did anything that even resembled punishment for chasing it would be construed by Fifi as punishment for coming to you and would discourage her from coming the next time.

SUMMARY

1. Dogs learn through pleasant and unpleasant experiences.
2. A behavior not rewarded is soon forgotten.

Don't discourage your dog from coming to you.

3. Good training rewards the desired behavior and discourages or ignores the undesired behavior.
4. Stop rewarding undesired behaviors.
5. Do not punish your dog for coming to you.
6. Always reward your dog for coming to you.

Necessary items for housetraining.

5

Housetraining

KEYS to successful housetraining are:

1. crate-train your puppy (see chapter 6)
2. set a schedule for feeding and exercising your dog
3. stick to that schedule, even on weekends, at least until your dog is housetrained and mature
4. be vigilant, vigilant and vigilant until your dog is trained.

Using a crate to housetrain your puppy is the most humane and effective way. It is also the easiest because of the dog's natural desire to keep its den clean.

THE PUPPY

Puppies have to eliminate two to three times more frequently than adult dogs in a twenty-four-hour period. A puppy's ability to control elimination increases with age, from not at all to up to eight hours and more. During the day, when active, the puppy can last for only short periods. Until it is six months of age, it is unrealistic to expect it to last for more than four hours during the day without having to eliminate. When sleeping, most puppies can last through the night.

Stick to the schedule.

Setting a schedule

Dogs and puppies thrive on a regular routine. By feeding and exercising your dog at about the same time every day, your pup will also relieve itself at about the same time every day.

Set a time to feed the puppy that is convenient for you. Always feed at the same time. Until four months of age, a dog needs four meals a day; from four to seven months, three meals. From then on feed *twice* a day—it is healthier than feeding only once and helps with housetraining.

Feeding Schedule

Age	Feed
7 through 16 weeks	4 times a day
17 through 28 weeks	3 times a day
29 weeks and over	2 times a day

40

Feed the right amount—loose stools are a sign of overfeeding, straining or dry stools a sign of underfeeding. After ten minutes, pick up the food dish and put it away. Do not have food available at other times. Keep the diet constant. Abrupt changes of food may cause digestive upsets that will not help your housetraining efforts.

Fresh water must be available to your dog during the day. You can put away the water dish after 8:00 P.M. so the pup can last through the night.

Establish a toilet area

Start by selecting a toilet area and always go to that spot when you want your dog to eliminate. If possible, pick a place in a straight line from the house. Carry your puppy or put it on leash. Stand still so the dog can concentrate on eliminating. Teach a command, such as "hurry up." Be patient; let the pup sniff around. Afterward, lavishly praise your puppy and go back inside.

Sample schedule

First thing in the morning, Mary takes her twelve-week-old Poodle puppy, Colette, out of the crate and straight outside to the toilet area. Fifteen minutes after Colette's morning meal, she is let out again. Mary then crates Colette and leaves for work.

Establish a toilet area.

Sample schedule.

On her lunch break, Mary goes home to let Colette out to relieve herself, feeds her and then, just to make sure, takes her out once more. For the afternoon, Colette is crated again until Mary returns. Colette is then walked and fed, after which she spends the rest of the evening in the house where Mary can keep an eye on her. Before bedtime, Colette goes out to the toilet area one more time and is then crated for the night.

When Colette becomes seven months old, Mary will drop the noontime feeding and walk. From then on, most dogs only need to go out immediately or soon after waking up in the morning, late afternoon and once again before bedtime.

Vigilance

Take your puppy to its toilet area after eating or drinking, after waking up and after playing. Another sign that your dog has to go out is sniffing the ground and circling in a small area.

Special vigilance is required when it is raining because many

Take your puppy out after . . .

dogs, particularly those with short hair, do not like to go out in the wet any more than you do. Make sure the puppy actually eliminates before you bring it back into the house.

DEALING WITH ACCIDENTS

When your dog has had an accident in the house, *do not* call Spot to you to punish him. It is too late. If you do punish your dog under these circumstances it will not help your housetraining efforts and you will make the dog wary of wanting to come to you.

There is a popular misconception that Spot "knows" what he did because he looks "guilty." *Absolutely not so*. He has that look because from prior experience he knows that when you come across a mess, you get angry. Your dog learned to associate a mess with your angry response. He cannot perceive the connection between making the mess in the first place and your anger.

Swatting your dog with a rolled-up newspaper is cruel and only creates fear of you and rolled-up newspapers. Rubbing the dog's nose in the mess is unsanitary and disgusting.

Dogs become housetrained in spite of such tactics and not because of them.

When you come upon an accident, always keep calm. Put Spot out of sight so he cannot watch you clean up. Use white vinegar as cleaner. Do not use any ammonia-based cleaners since the ammonia does not neutralize the odor and the puppy will be attracted to the same place.

Catching your dog in the act

If you catch your dog in the act, sharply call the pup's name and clap your hands. If the dog stops, go to your dog's toilet area. If not, don't get mad. Do not try to drag the dog out because that will make your cleanup job that much more difficult.

Hint: Until your puppy is reliable, it is not a good idea to allow free run of the house unsupervised.

Regressions

Regressions *will* occur, especially during teething. Regressions well after six months of age may be a sign that your dog is ill. If accidents persist, visit your veterinarian.

SUMMARY

1. Using a crate to housetrain your puppy is the most humane and effective way.
2. When active, puppies can last for only short periods before they have to eliminate.
3. Dogs thrive on a regular routine of feeding and exercising at the same time every day.
4. It is healthier for your dog to feed twice a day rather than once.
5. Take your puppy to its toilet area after eating or drinking, after waking up and after playing or chewing.
6. When your dog has had an accident in the house, do not call your dog to you to give out punishment.

A crate is like having a baby-sitter for your dog.

6

A "Baby-sitter" for Your Dog

W HEN RITA AND TED went to pick up their puppy, the breeder asked them what they thought was a peculiar question. "When you were raising your children, did you use a playpen?"

"Of course," said Rita. "I don't know what I would have done without it."

"Fine," said Christine. "A crate for a puppy is like a playpen for a child."

Whatever your views on playpens, dogs like crates. It reminds them of a den—a place of safety, security and warmth. Puppies, and many adult dogs, sleep most of the day, and they prefer the comfort of their den.

For your sanity and the puppy's safety, get a crate for your dog.

Here are just a few of the many advantages of crate-training your dog:

1. When you are busy and can't keep an eye on Ms. Goodpuppy, but want to make sure she will not get into trouble, put her in a crate. You can relax and so can she.
2. Crates are ideal for establishing a schedule for housetraining.
3. Few dogs are fortunate enough to go through life without ever

having to be hospitalized. Your dog's private room at the veterinary hospital will consist of a crate. First experience with a crate should not come at a time when the dog is sick, as the added stress from being crated for the first time will retard recovery. There may also be times when you have to keep your dog quiet, such as after an injury or being altered.

4. Driving any distance, even around the block, with your dog loose in the car is tempting fate. If you make an emergency

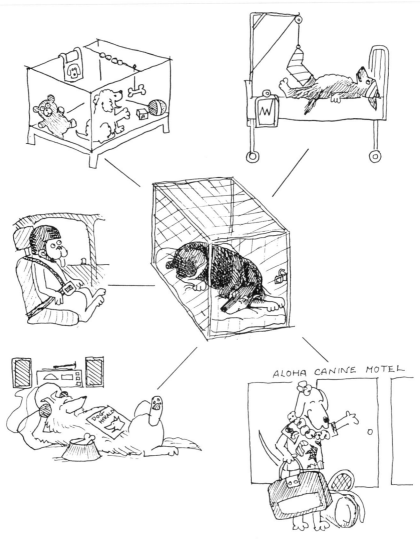

Crate-training has many advantages.

stop, who knows what will happen? Having the dog in a crate protects you and your dog.

5. When we go on vacation we like to take our dog. A crate is a home away from home, and we can leave Princess in a hotel room knowing she won't be unhappy or stressed or try to tear up the room.
6. Most important for your dog, the crate is a place where she can get away from the hustle and bustle of family life and hide out when the kids become too much.

Your dog will like the crate because it will remind her of the security of a den. She will use it voluntarily, so she should always have access to it. Depending on where it is, your dog will spend a lot of sleeping time in the crate.

SELECTING A CRATE

Select a crate that is large enough so your dog can turn around, stand or lie down comfortably. Even if the dog is still a puppy, get a crate for the adult-size dog.

Some crates are better than others in ease of assembly and strength. You can get crates of wire mesh–type material or of plastic, called airline crates. Most are designed for portability and are easily assembled.

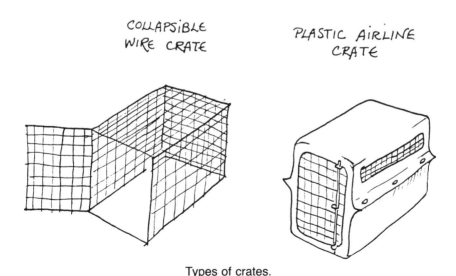

COLLAPSIBLE WIRE CRATE

PLASTIC AIRLINE CRATE

Types of crates.

We recommend a good-quality crate that collapses easily and is portable so you can take it with you when traveling with your dog. If you frequently take your dog with you in the car, consider getting two crates, one for the house and one for the car. It will save you having to lug one back and forth.

INTRODUCING THE CRATE

Set up the crate and let your dog investigate it. Choose a command, such as "crate," or "go to bed." Physically place your dog in the crate using the command you have chosen. Tell her what a great little puppy she is, give her a bite-sized treat, and let her out.

Next, use a treat to coax her into the crate.

If she does not follow the treat, physically place her into the crate and then give the treat.

Introduction to the crate.

Do this until the puppy goes into the crate with almost no help from you, each time using the command and giving a treat *after* she is in the crate.

For the puppy that is afraid of the crate, use meals to overcome fear. First, let her eat the meal in front of the crate, then place the next meal just inside the crate. Put each successive meal a little further into the crate until she is completely inside and no longer reluctant to go in.

Getting puppy used to the crate

Tell your dog to go into the crate, give her a treat, close the door and tell her what a good puppy she is, then let her out again. Each time you do this, leave Princess in the crate a little longer with the door closed, still giving a treat and telling her how great she is.

Finally, put her in the crate, give a treat and then leave the room, first for five minutes, then ten minutes, then fifteen minutes and so on. Each time you return to let her out, tell Princess how good she was before you open the door.

How long can you ultimately leave your dog in a crate unattended? That depends on your dog and your schedule, but it should not be more than the length of a workday.

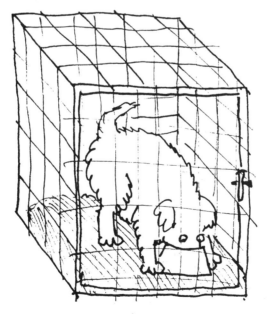

Feeding your puppy in the crate.

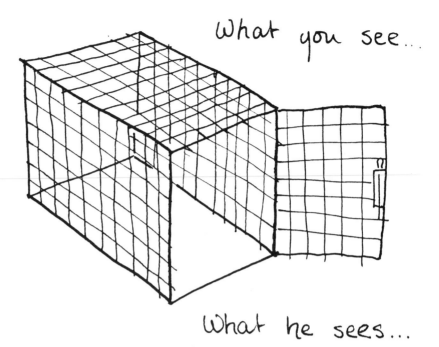

What you see...

What he sees...

Your dog's perception of a crate.

A WORD OF CAUTION

A crate should never be used as a form of punishment. If it is, your dog will begin to dislike the crate and it will lose its usefulness to you. The old "go to your room without supper" approach does not work any better with dogs than it does with children.

SUMMARY

1. For your sanity and your puppy's safety, get a crate.
2. A crate reminds your dog of a den.
3. Dogs like the safety and security of a crate.
4. Among its many advantages, a crate is ideal for housetraining.
5. When traveling with your dog in the car, for her safety and yours, put Princess in her crate.
6. A crate is never used as a form of punishment.

In polite company, the sit and stay is essential.

7

Sit and Stay

DIFFERENT STYLES of greetings have been perfected by dogs. Bart, the Lab, would launch himself about six feet from his owner, who did not appreciate having to catch this missile.

JUMPING ON PEOPLE

The question almost every dog owner asks is "How do I keep my dog from jumping up on people?"

Dogs jump on people as a form of greeting, like saying "hello, nice to meet you!" Even the briefest of separations from the owner, as little as five minutes, can set off this behavior.

As annoying as it may be at times, please remember that greeting is a gesture of affection and good will. We certainly do not recommend any form of punishment to deal with it.

So how do you get your dog Bean to stop without dampening his enthusiasm? By teaching him to sit and stay on command. Your dog can't jump on you when he is sitting—the two behaviors are mutually exclusive.

SAFETY

Equally annoying, but far more dangerous, is the dog's habit of dashing through doors just because they are open. It is dangerous

Greeting behavior without training.

Sit and stay is important for safety.

because Bean may find himself in the middle of the road and get run over, or, if you are in the process of opening a door, he may knock you down as he rushes through.

Such potential accidents can be prevented by teaching your dog to sit and stay while you open the door and to wait until you say "OK, go out."

Sit and stay also applies to getting in and out of the car as well as going up and down stairs. We never liked the thought of having both arms full while going down a staircase with a dog dashing by.

When the doorbell rings, you can tell Bean to sit and stay while you answer it instead of having him frantically charge the door.

All these maneuvers can be performed smoothly and without worry, once you have taught your dog to sit and stay.

The sit and stay is one of the simplest and yet most useful exercises you can teach your dog. It gives you a wonderfully easy way to control your pet when you need it most.

Sit and stay is used when you want your dog to remain quietly in one spot for a *short* time. For example, Keno, a German Shepherd, would become so excited when Sally was about to feed him that he sent the dish flying out of her hands. Once taught the sit and stay, he sat like a perfect gentleman while she put the dish down.

COMMANDS TO BE TAUGHT

You are going to teach your dog three commands:

1. sit
2. stay
3. OK.

OK is the release command. It means Bean can move now and do whatever he wants, almost. Make it a strict rule that you give the release command, after every time you have told Bean to stay, when he is allowed to move again. Should you get lax about it and forget, Bean will get into the habit of releasing himself and learn that *he* can decide when to move, the opposite of what *you* want.

Unless impaired, a dog's sense of hearing is extremely acute, so when giving a command there is absolutely no need to shout. Commands are given in a normal tone of voice, such as "sit!" "Sit!" is the command and not "sit?" the question. The release word "OK" is

Before and after learning the sit.

given in a more excited tone of voice, to convey "that's it, you're all done."

When teaching a new command, you may have to repeat it several times before your dog catches on. When you are past that initial stage, teach Bean to respond to the first command. Give the command and if nothing happens, show your dog exactly what it is you want by physically helping him. Consistency is the key to success.

Teaching your dog to sit on command

Your dog already knows how to sit. What he has to learn is what you expect from him when you say "sit" and to obey every time you give him the command.

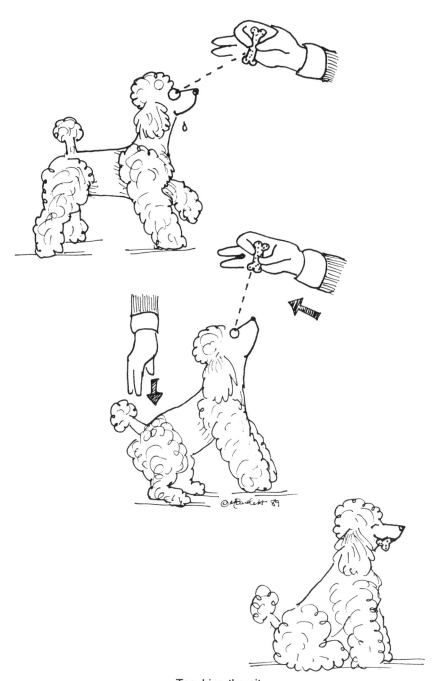

Teaching the sit.

Begin by showing Bean a small, bite-sized treat, holding it just a little in front of his eyes, slightly over his head. Say "sit" as you bring your hand above his eyes. Looking up at the treat will cause your dog to sit. When he does, give the treat and tell him what a good puppy he is. Tell him without petting him. If you pet as you praise him, he will probably get up when you really want him to sit.

Study the illustration on page 59 for the position of your hand in relation to your dog's head. If your hand is held too high, your dog will jump up; if it is too low, he will not sit.

If Bean does not respond on his own, say "sit" again and press *lightly* on his rump with your other hand to get him to sit, and then give the treat.

Practice making your dog sit five times in a row for five days. Some dogs catch on to this idea so quickly that whenever they want a treat they sit in front of their owner.

When Bean understands what "sit" means, you can start to teach him to obey your command. Put your hand through his collar at the top of the neck, palm facing up, and tell him to sit. If he does, give him a treat and tell him how good he is; if he does not, pull up on the collar, wait until he sits and praise and reward with a treat.

Practice until he sits on command, that is, without your having to pull up on or touch the collar. Give a treat and praise with "good puppy" for *every* correct response.

When he sits on command *only,* reward the desired response

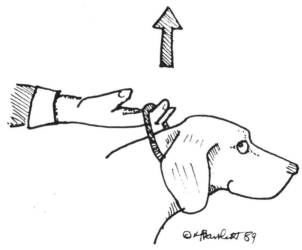

Teach your pup to obey the command "sit."

Sitting to be petted.

every other time. Finally, reward on a random basis—every now and then give a treat after he sits on command. A random reward is the most powerful reinforcement of what your dog has learned. It is based on the simple premise that hope springs eternal. To make it work, all you have to do is use it and keep using it!

Now, when Bean wants to greet you by jumping up, tell him to sit. Bend down, briefly pet him and tell him what a good puppy he is, then release him. By following this simple method consistently, you will have changed your dog's greeting behavior from trying to jump on you to sitting to be petted.

Teaching your dog to stay

An easy way to teach your dog to understand the stay command is to make him sit and stay for his supper. As you are getting ready to feed, bowl in hand, say "sit," "stay" and lower the bowl to the ground. As your pup starts for it, pick up the bowl before he gets even a mouthful. Put him back where he was supposed to sit and stay. Start all over. Repeat until you can put the bowl down and count to five before saying "OK." Then let him eat in peace.

After several days of following this regimen, your dog will sit on his own when he sees you approaching with supper and wait until you say "OK." This is a much more pleasant way to feed your dog than having him jump up and down, trying to knock the dish out of your hands.

Once he will sit and stay for food, you are ready for the next important lesson: Wait until I tell you *before* you dash through that

Teaching the stay.

door. Start by sitting your dog in front of a closed door. You know that if you open the door Bean will want to go through. Tell him to stay and start opening the door. When he starts to get up, close the door, put him back in the exact spot where you said ''stay'' and start all over. If your dog is particularly fast or wiggly or very strong, use a leash as you begin. (For leash training, see chapter 9.)

You will find that after you have put your dog back three or four times he begins to get the message and will stay. With your dog on a stay, practice until you can open the door all the way before closing it again. From now on, every time you let Bean out, make him sit first, open the door, then release with ''OK.''

Get into the habit of having your dog sit and stay before you open any door. Some of us prefer to go through the doorway first, while others want the dog to go through first. It makes no difference, so long as Bean stays until you release him. Practice with doors your dog uses regularly, including the car doors. Every time you make him sit and stay it reinforces your position as pack leader and the one in charge.

If you have stairs, start teaching your dog to stay at the bottom while you go up. First sit him, then give the *stay* command. When he tries to follow, put him back and start again. Practice until you can go

Practical applications of the sit and stay.

all the way up the stairs with him waiting at the bottom before you release him to follow.

Repeat the same procedure going down the stairs.

Once your dog has been trained to wait at one end of the stairs, you will discover that he will anticipate the release. He will jump the gun and get up just as you are thinking of releasing him. Before long, he will only stay briefly and release when *he* chooses. It may happen almost as soon as he has grasped the idea or it may take a few weeks or even months, but it *will* happen.

When it does, stop whatever you are doing and put him back, count to ten and release. *Do not let him get into the habit of releasing himself.* Consistency is just as important here as in any other exercise.

SUMMARY

1. "Sit and stay" is used when you want your dog to remain quietly in one spot for a short time.
2. When your dog sits on command, it cannot jump on you.
3. "Sit and stay" applies to going through doors, up and down stairs and in and out of the car.
4. A random reward is the most powerful reinforcement of what your dog has learned.
5. After you have given the stay command, remember to release—make it a strict rule.
6. Unless you periodically reinforce the stay, your dog will begin to release automatically.

8

Go Lie Down

Now THAT YOUR DOG RESPONDS to "sit," she is ready for the next lesson: to lie down on command.

COMMANDS TO BE TAUGHT

You are going to teach your dog two new commands:

1. Go lie down
2. Down.

"Go lie down" is used when you want your dog to remain quietly in one place for a *long* time, from five minutes up to one hour. It is most commonly used when you are eating or when friends visit and you don't want your dog making a pest of herself. When you give the command, she is expected to go to a favorite spot and get comfortable. When she can get up again, release her.

"Down" is used when you want her to lie down in place right now and stay there until you give a release command.

Teaching your dog to lie down on command

Again, your dog already knows how to lie down. What you are going to teach her is to do it when *you* tell her.

This dog needs to learn "go lie down."

First, sit your dog at your left side. Put two fingers of your left hand, palm facing you, through the collar at the side of her neck. Have a treat in your right hand. Show the treat and lower it straight down and in front of your dog as you apply downward pressure on the collar, at the same time saying "down." When she lies down, give the treat and praise by telling her what a good puppy she is. Keep your left hand in the collar and your right hand off your puppy while telling her how clever she is so she learns to be praised for lying down. With a small dog you may want to use a table for training.

Reverse the process by showing a treat and bringing it up slightly above her head with upward pressure on the collar as you tell her to "sit."

Look at the illustration opposite and study the way the right hand moves down and in front of your dog in an L shape, and the position of the left hand. Hint: Place the treat between the dog's front legs.

Practice having your dog lie down at your side five times in a row for five days, or until she does it on command with minimal pressure on the collar. Praise and reward with a treat every time.

When she understands what the word means, you can move on to

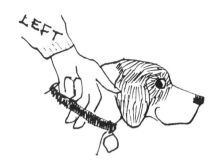

Teaching the down.

the next step. Sit your dog at your left side and put two fingers of your left hand, palm facing you, through the collar at the side of her neck. Say "down" and apply downward pressure on the collar. When your dog lies down, praise and give a treat every *other* time. Practice over the course of several days until she will lie down on command without any pressure on the collar.

After that, when she lies down on command, randomly reward as explained in chapter 7.

Teaching your dog to remain in place

You can now start to teach your dog to lie down in one place for several minutes. Sit in a chair and have your dog sit at your left side. Tell her to lie down; if necessary, place her down with a little pressure on the collar and the command "down." Keep an eye on her and when she tries to get up, place her down again. Teach the stay in the down position for five minutes, then praise and release with "OK."

Practicing the response to "down."

If your dog is very bouncy, you may want to put her on leash and then sit on the leash so your hands are free to put your dog in position.

As she learns the stay in the down position, gradually and over the course of several sessions increase the time until she will stay up to thirty minutes before you release.

There is no need to tell your dog to stay since she will learn that "down" or "go lie down" includes stay until released. You do have to remember to release your dog so she does not just get up at will, which would defeat the object of the exercise.

Once she understands what is expected and you use "go lie down," make sure she responds to the first command you give. If she doesn't, stop what you are doing and place her down.

Be persistent in teaching a dog to remain in the down position.

SUMMARY

1. "Go lie down" is used when you want your dog to remain quietly in one place for long periods of time.
2. "Down" is used when you want her to lie down in place, right now.
3. Down is another exercise that teaches your dog you are in charge.
4. Be sure you release her so that she does not get into the habit of releasing at will.

9

Walking Your Dog

TAKING YOUR DOG for a nice, long walk is balm for the soul and good exercise for both of you, provided your dog does not drag you down the street.

Even if you don't ordinarily go for walks, it is still a good idea to teach your pet some manners while on leash. For example, at least once a year you will have to go to the veterinarian. If your dog has been trained to walk on leash, the visit will go much more smoothly than if the animal bounces off the end of the leash like a kangaroo. Of course, if the dog is small, you can always carry it.

Most of us want to be able to take the dog for a walk within the length of the leash without pulling. A leisurely stroll is an important daily routine, and for many dogs the only opportunity to get some fresh air.

LEASH-TRAINING YOUR DOG

Before you can start the section on teaching your dog not to pull, you will need to get Rocky accustomed to wearing a collar and walking on a leash.

From your local pet supply outlet purchase an adjustable buckle collar of fabric or leather, and a six-foot canvas or nylon leash. Take your puppy's neck measurement before you go. The collar should be

Teach your dog to *walk* on leash.

snug, about as snug as a turtleneck sweater, high on the neck and *just behind the ears,* so that he cannot slip out of it. As Rocky grows, you may have to buy a larger collar later on.

Fasten the collar around his neck and see what he does. Most puppies show little reaction to a collar. Some will scratch their neck at first, but as they become accustomed to wearing the collar, they ignore it.

When he is used to the collar, attach the leash and let him drag it around. You will need to supervise so that he does not get tangled. Once he ignores the leash, pick up the other end and follow him around. He will happily wander off wherever his fancy takes him.

You are now ready to show him where you want to go. First use a treat to make him follow you and then gently guide him with the leash, saying what a good puppy he is. If you are teaching outside, use the treat to coax him away from the house and the leash to guide him back toward the house.

Before you know it, he will not only walk on the leash in your direction, but actually pull you along.

TEACHING YOUR DOG NOT TO PULL

To teach Rocky not to pull, you need a collar, a leash and a few treats. Decide where you want him to walk in relation to you—the traditional position is at your left side.

How seriously you approach training will depend on how often you plan taking Rocky for a walk and for what purpose. If you like to take him along while you jog or go for a brisk walk, then he has to learn to stay at your side so *you* don't trip.

If you walk only so that he can relieve himself, it matters little where he is in relation to you, so long as he does not pull.

Go to an area without too many distractions (such as other people and dogs, especially loose dogs) and where you can walk in a circle about thirty feet in diameter.

Hold the leash in both hands, say "let's go" and start walking. When Rocky tries to get ahead of you or begins to pull on the leash, say "easy" and bring him back to your left side with a tug on the leash. When he walks where you want him to, praise by saying "what a good puppy" and give a treat!

You will have to repeat this several times over the course of a few training sessions until he understands where you want him in relation to you and that you don't want him to pull.

Your initial goal is to be able to walk for ten steps without Rocky pulling on the leash. Next, practice until you can walk him on a loose leash for thirty steps, then sixty and, finally, the entire circle.

Once your dog has mastered the circle, try changing direction and reward with a treat when he stays at your side.

You are now ready to take your dog for a walk down the street. At first, you may find that you have to remind Rocky occasionally where you want him to be, especially if you meet another dog. Using your "easy" command and the tug on the leash will teach him not to pull, even when there are distractions.

ALTERNATIVE

If you find your dog ignores your tugs or, worse yet, drags you the length of a football field and your arms are now two inches longer, try a head halter.

Your dog may need several practice sessions to get used to it, but

Teaching your dog not to pull.

once he accepts it he will readily respond to the training. The head halter is based on the principle that where the dog's head goes, the body has to follow.

Note: The head halter is to be used only when walking or training your dog.

If your pet supply outlet does not carry this item, it can order the halter for you or advise you where to purchase one.

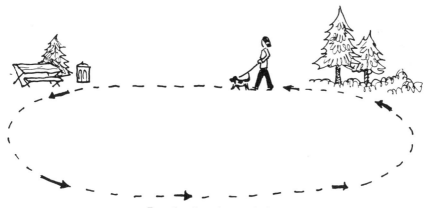

Practice in a large circle.

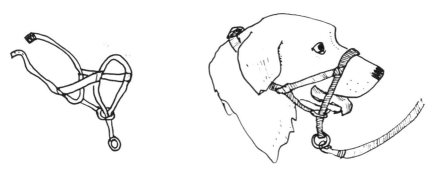

Alternative: a head halter.

SUMMARY

1. It is a good idea to teach your dog to walk on a leash without pulling.
2. How seriously you approach training will depend on how often you plan on taking the dog for a walk.
3. Use a treat and verbal praise when the dog does it correctly.
4. Be patient and maintain a friendly and positive attitude toward your dog.
5. If you can't seem to get anywhere, consider a change of equipment.

The most useful command in dog training: "come when called."

10

Coming When Called

ONE OF THE GREATEST JOYS of owning a dog is to go for a walk in a park or the woods and let your animal run, knowing it will come when called. A dog that does not come when called is a prisoner of the leash and, if loose, a danger to itself and others.

If your dog does not come when called, you don't have a dog!

The joy of a dog that comes when called.

Exercise needs vary.

Rule 1 Exercise, exercise, exercise.

Many dogs do not come when called because they do not get enough exercise. At every chance, they run off and make the most of it by staying out for hours at a time.

Consider what your dog was bred to do and that will tell you how much exercise it needs. Just putting Konrad out in the backyard will not do. You will have to participate. Think of it this way: Exercise is as good for you as it is for your dog.

Rule 2 Whenever your dog comes to you, be nice.

One of the quickest ways to teach your dog *not* to come to you is to call him for punishment or to do something the dog perceives as unpleasant. Most dogs consider being given a bath or a pill unpleasant. When Konrad needs either, go and get him instead of calling him to you.

Another example of teaching your dog not to come is to take him for a run in the park and call him to you when it's time to go home. Repeating this sequence several times teaches the dog "the party is over!" Soon, Konrad may become reluctant to return to you when called because he is not ready to end the fun.

You can prevent this kind of unintentional training by calling

If your dog dislikes baths, go and get him, but don't call him to you.

your dog to you several times during the outing, sometimes giving a treat, sometimes just a pat on the head. Then let him romp again.

Rule 3   Teach Konrad to come when called as soon as you bring the pup home, no matter how young he is.

Ideally, you acquired your dog as a puppy, and that is the best time to teach him to come when called. Start right away. But remember, sometime between the fourth and eighth months of age, your puppy will begin to realize there is a big, wide world out there (see chapter 2).

While going through this stage, keep the pup on leash so that he does not learn to ignore you when you call.

Rule 4   When in doubt, keep your dog on leash.

Learn to anticipate when your dog is likely *not* to come. You may be tempting fate trying to call once he has spotted a cat, another dog or a jogger. Of course, there will be times when you goof and let him go just as another dog appears out of nowhere.

Resist the urge to make a complete fool of yourself by bellowing "come" a million times. The more often you holler "come," the quicker he learns to ignore you when he is off leash. Instead, patiently go to him and put Konrad on leash. Do not get angry once you have caught him or you will make him afraid; then he will run away when you try to catch him the next time.

Coming to you need not be the end of play.

Rule 5   Make sure your dog always comes to you and lets you touch his collar *before* you reward with a treat or praise.

Touching the collar prevents the dog from developing the annoying habit of playing "catch"—coming toward you and then dancing around you, just out of reach.

THE GAME OF COMING WHEN CALLED

Needed: two people, one hungry dog, one six-foot leash and plenty of small treats.

Teach your dog to come as soon as you get him.

Step 1: Inside the house, with your dog on a six-foot leash, you and your partner sit on the floor or ground, six feet apart, facing each other. Your partner gently hangs on to the dog, you hold the end of the leash. Call your dog by saying ''Konrad, come,'' and use the leash to guide the pup to you. Put your hand through the collar, give a treat, pet and praise him enthusiastically.

    Now you hold the dog and pass the leash to your partner, who says ''Konrad, come,'' guides the dog in, puts a hand through the collar, gives a treat and praises the dog.

Goal: Repeat until your dog responds voluntarily to being called and no longer needs to be guided in with the leash.

When in doubt, keep your dog on leash.

Touch the collar before giving a reward for coming.

Step 2: Repeat step 1 with your dog off leash.

Goal: Gradually increase the distance between you and your partner to twelve feet.

Step 3: Have your partner hold your dog (off leash) while you hide

The recall game—step 1.

from Konrad (go into another room), then call your dog. When he finds you, put your hand through the collar, give a treat and praise. If he can't find you, go to him, take the collar and bring him to the spot where you called. Reward and praise. Now have your partner hide and then call your dog.

Goal: Repeat until the dog doesn't hesitate in finding you or your partner in any room of the house.

GOING OUTSIDE

Take your dog outside to a confined area, such as a fenced yard, tennis court, park or schoolyard and repeat steps 1, 2 and 3.

You are now ready to practice by yourself. Let Konrad loose in a confined area and ignore him. When he is not paying any attention to you, call. When he gets to you, give a treat and make a big fuss. If he does not come, go to him, take his collar and bring him to the spot where you called and then reward and praise him.

Repeat until Konrad comes to you every time you call.

Once your dog is trained, you don't have to reward with a treat every time, but do so frequently.

The recall game—step 3.

ADDING DISTRACTIONS

Some dogs will need to be trained to come in the face of distractions such as other dogs, children, joggers, food or friendly strangers. Think about the most irresistible situations for your dog and then practice under those circumstances.

On-leash distractions

Step 1: Put a twelve-foot leash on your dog (this can be two six-foot leashes tied together) and go to an area where you are likely to encounter his favorite distraction (jogger, bicycle, other dog, whatever). Once he's distracted, let him become thoroughly engrossed, either by watching or straining at the leash, and give the command "Konrad, come." More than likely, he will ignore you. Give a sharp tug on the leash and guide him back to you. Praise and pet him enthusiastically.

Practicing outside.

Practice with distractions, on leash.

Goal: Repeat three times per session until the dog turns and comes to you immediately when you call. If he does not, you may have to change your training equipment. (See chapter 9.)

Note: Some dogs quickly learn to avoid the distraction by staying close to you, which is fine. Tell Konrad what a clever fellow he is and then try with a different distraction at another time.

Step 2: Repeat step 1 in different locations with as many different distractions as you can find. Try it with someone offering your dog a *tidbit as a distraction (the dog is not* to get the treat), someone petting the dog and anything else that may distract him. Use your imagination.Goal: A dog that comes immediately when called, even when distracted.

Off-leash distractions

How you approach this part of the training will depend on your individual circumstances. Here is an example.

Teaching your dog to respond off leash.

Take your dog to an area where you are not likely to encounter distractions in the form of other dogs or people. Remove the leash and let Konrad become involved in smelling the grass or a tree. Keep the distance between you and him about ten feet. Call him. If he responds, praise enthusiastically. If not, avoid the temptation to call him again. Don't worry; he heard you, but chose to ignore you. Instead, slowly walk up behind him, firmly take the collar under his chin, palm up, and trot backward to the spot where you called from. Then praise.

Once Konrad is reliable at this point, try an area with other distractions. If he does not respond, practice for the correct response with the twelve-foot leash before you try off leash again.

Can you now trust him to come in an unconfined area? That will depend on how well you have done your homework and what your dog may encounter in the real world. Understanding your dog and what

Let common sense be your guide.

interests him will help you know when he is not likely to respond to being called.

Let common sense be your guide. For example, when you are traveling and have to let your dog out at a busy interstate rest stop, it would be foolhardy to do so off leash. Remember the rule: When in doubt, keep the leash on.

SUMMARY

1. If your dog does not come when called, you don't have a dog.
2. Whenever your dog comes to you, be nice.
3. When in doubt, keep the leash on.
4. Always touch the collar after your dog comes to you and before you give a reward.
5. Teach your dog to come when called *now*.
6. "Come" is the most important command you will teach your dog.

11

Objectionable Behavior

IF YOU HAVE FOLLOWED THE ADVICE in the previous chapters, you may never need this one! If you have skipped the first part of this book and turned immediately to this chapter, go back and start at the beginning. Most dogs respond well to basic training, and many objectionable behaviors can be resolved that way. That's the main purpose of training.

In the event some problem persists, you have several options:

1. tolerate it
2. train
3. find a new home for your dog
4. euthanize the dog.

Tolerate it.

At first blush this may not seem like much of an option. Then you begin to consider the amount of time and energy that could be involved in dealing with your dog's annoying antics and you may decide that you can live with them after all. You tolerate the way the dog is because you are not prepared to put in the required effort to change it.

Train!

You have decided that you cannot live with such behavior and that you are going to train your dog to be the pet you expected and always wanted. You understand this will require an initial investment of time and effort, perhaps even expert help. But you are willing to work to achieve your goal—a long-lasting, mutually rewarding relationship. Good for you!

For most of us, dog ownership is a compromise between *tolerate* and *train*. Our Standard Wirehaired Dachshund, Demi, is housebroken, crate-trained, comes when called (mostly) and stays when told. All this training has not shaken her conviction that her purpose on this earth is to practice her landscaping skills, which she does with enthusiasm and determination. We, in turn, have learned to tolerate her efforts.

Find a new home for your dog.

Your dog's temperament may be unsuitable to your life-style. A shy dog, or a dog with physical limitations, may never develop into a great playmate for active children. A dog that does not like to be left alone too long would not be suitable for someone who is gone all day. While some behaviors can be modified with training, others cannot, or the effort required would make a neurotic out of the dog.

In some instances the dog and the owner are mismatched and they need to divorce. The dog may need a great deal more exercise than the owner is able to give, and as a result the dog is developing behavior problems. Whatever the reason, under some circumstances placement in a new home where the dog's needs can be met is advisable and in the best interest of both dog and owner.

Euthanize the dog.

If all reclamation efforts have failed, you can't live with this dog and the dog can't be placed because it is dangerous or for some other reason, another option is euthanasia. It is not something to be taken lightly, and should be considered only when you have really tried to work it out and there are truly no other alternatives. Veterinarians do not take this lightly either and most will not euthanize a dog that is not dangerous or seriously ill.

These are your options.

WHY DOES YOUR DOG DO IT?

Many owners believe their dogs misbehave out of spite. They are indignant at what they perceive to be the dog's lack of gratitude. After all, "I house you, I feed you, I take care of all your veterinary expenses, the least you can do is not chew up my shoes!" Unfortunately, dogs are not grateful and don't know what the word means.

Dogs do not lie awake at night thinking up mischief:
There is a reason for problem behavior.

When your dog barks, chews, digs or whatever, the activity is rewarding in and of itself. Your dog does not lie awake at night thinking of ways to aggravate you, but acts to satisfy a need. For example, barking, chewing and digging are associated with boredom and tension. The dog engages in the particular behavior because the activity relieves the boredom or tension. It can also be attention-getting behavior. For a dog that wants attention almost anything, even being scolded, is better than no attention at all.

The easiest way to stop a behavior is by dealing with the need that brought it about in the first place, rather than trying to correct the behavior itself. Punitive approaches cause your dog to be afraid of you and undermine the very relationship you are trying to build.

So-called behavior problems are often the effect of some cause and not a cause in and of itself. Find the cause, and you will have cured the problem. Lack of sufficient exercise, isolation and mental stagnation, health and nutrition problems and unintentional training are the main causes for a variety of objectionable behaviors.

Lack of sufficient exercise

This is the most common reason for objectionable behavior. A Vizsla is a hunting dog with a high energy level. Cooped up in a house all day, the dog may take to shredding the couch to get rid of that energy. What is sufficient for your dog depends on age, size, breed and

Lack of sufficient exercise.

93

Isolation and mental stagnation.

energy level, but it is actually much more than you think. A trained dog is a happy dog, and a tired one is even happier.

Isolation and mental stagnation

Your dog does not need you as a full-time entertainment center, but extended periods of being left alone will make your pet a neurotic. Problems associated with isolation are excessive barking, chewing and digging, and self-mutilation.

Dogs are pack animals and need interaction with the "pack" members, that is, you and your family. Just being together is often enough, but training is even better. Doing something for you on a

Make your dog feel useful.

regular basis makes your dog feel useful and provides the mental stimulation that is so needed.

Being left alone too long can result in separation anxiety which in turn results in destructive chewing or similar unwanted actions. Often it is created by making a big fuss before leaving the dog. The dog is left in an empty house in a state of high excitement which is relieved by chewing or barking.

Instead, ignore the dog before you leave and then leave for short

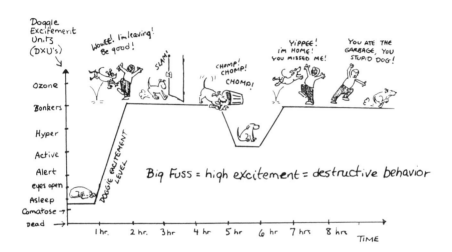

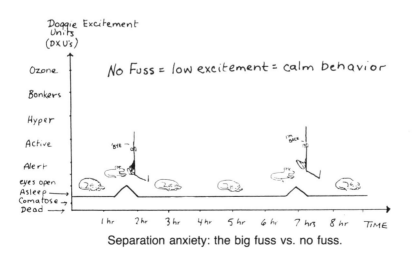

Separation anxiety: the big fuss vs. no fuss.

periods without saying or doing anything—just leave. Return the same way—low key and ignoring the dog for the first five minutes. As the dog becomes accustomed to being left, increase the time. Becoming used to the routine, your dog will view the separation as a normal part of a day and nothing to cause any excitement.

Physical or health problems

These are the leading causes for a sudden change in behavior. A normally obedient dog suddenly refusing to sit, for example, may have developed arthritis, a spinal disorder or infected or impacted anal glands.

Physical problems are often the cause of aggression and biting. If biting is a problem, you *must* do something about it because it is only a matter of time before you face legal difficulties. Take your dog to a veterinarian for a thorough checkup. If nothing turns up and the behavior continues, you need help. (See pages 99–102.)

Improper diet

Diet can be responsible for aggression, as well as for hyperactivity and difficulty in housetraining. You need to consult your veterinarian to find out if your dog has allergies to substances contained in

Health problems.

dog food. These can range from chemical additives and food coloring to one or more of the main ingredients. Your dog may also have nutritional deficiencies.

Unintentional training

Biting behavior can also be triggered by roughhousing with your dog; teasing by children; tug-of-war games; mistreatment; tension or violence in the household; or fear or dominance on the part of the dog.

Roughhousing is a particularly dangerous form of ''play.'' Brandy started out as a sweet puppy. The children delighted in playing with her and she never caused any difficulties. Dad even took her to obedience class where she graduated at the top of her class.

Improper diet.

Unintentional training.

Several months later, problems developed. While being taken for a walk by Mom, Brandy started a tug-of-war with the leash. When Mom tried to get her to stop, Brandy growled. She also became too rough for the children, who now did not want to play with her anymore.

When Dad called with this sad tale asking for advice, it did not take too long to learn that he liked to roughhouse and play tug-of-war with Brandy. He saw nothing wrong with it since he was able to keep Brandy under control when things got too rough. We explained to him that he had taught Brandy to become rougher and rougher, but that Mom and the children could not control her. He was to stop all the rough play and review the obedience exercises.

Fortunately for Brandy, the story has a happy ending. Once Dad quit the fooling around and spent more constructive time with her, Brandy became her sweet old self again.

Put another way, good behavior requires

1. good exercise
2. good company
3. good health
4. good nutrition
5. good training.

WHAT TO DO ABOUT UNACCEPTABLE BEHAVIOR

If you find a particular behavior unacceptable, find its cause and deal with it accordingly. Once you have ruled out the physical or dietary aspect, you can tackle the problem with exercise and training, which means spending more time with your dog. If despite your best efforts the problem persists, consult an expert.

In-house help

In-house help is an option, if you don't mind paying the price—it tends to be expensive. It works something like this: A consultant or trainer comes to your house, talks to you about your dog and then recommends a course of action that is expected to solve the problem.

Theoretically, it is the ideal solution to an owner's problem with the dog because the consultant or trainer can see firsthand what the dog is doing and make the appropriate recommendations.

If you are interested in the services of an in-house consultant or trainer, ask your veterinarian, who probably refers cases to such an

In-house training.

individual. As with all trainers, be sure to check the individual's training credentials thoroughly.

Boarding your dog to be trained

Another option, also expensive, is to send your dog to a facility that specializes in training. Three weeks is the customary minimum.

Training tends to be general obedience, which may or may not address your particular problem. For example, if Sherlock soils or shreds your drapes, that behavior needs to be dealt with in the environment where the drapes are.

Since your dog will stay at this facility, you have to be especially careful in its selection. Where will your dog be housed? What will be the daily schedule? How often will he be exercised? When and what do they feed? What methods will be used in training?

Finding the right place will not be easy. Whatever you do, inspect

Boarding your dog to be trained.

the facility and observe some of the training before you leave your dog, and ask for references.

Going to school with your dog

Another good option is to enroll in an obedience class. Although classes tend to be geared to teaching traditional obedience commands, such as heel, come and stay, most obedience instructors are able to advise you on a wide range of topics.

We are in favor of classes because they are economical and *get you involved in the training process*. Your dog also learns to behave around other dogs—*a tremendous advantage*.

Before you commit yourself to a class, attend one or two sessions and watch. Following are a few pointers to help you select a class:

Is the atmosphere friendly?

Do the dogs seem to enjoy the training?

Is the instructor pleasant and courteous to the human students in the class?

Does the instructor appear knowledgeable?

Do you like the way the dogs are being treated?

Would you want to treat *your* dog that way?

Do the dogs visibly progress in the training?

Going to school.

If you are not satisfied with what you see, visit another class. There are usually more than one and sometimes quite a few dog obedience groups that train in any given area. If you don't like the way one operates, try another; not all use the same approaches to training. It should not be difficult to find one that trains in accordance with your own personal values.

Presumably you have your dog because you like her; so train that way!

SUMMARY

1. In dealing with your dog's behavior, you have a variety of options, the most important one being training.
2. Dogs do not lie awake at night thinking of ways to aggravate their owners—they sleep just as you do.
3. To stop a behavior, address the need that brought it on in the first place.
4. Lack of sufficient exercise is the most common reason for objectionable behavior.
5. Good behavior requires good exercise, good company, good health, good nutrition and good training.
6. If you don't have the time or inclination to train your dog yourself, have someone do it for you.

12

Barking, Chewing and Digging

ALL OF THE BEHAVIORS discussed in this chapter present difficulties because they are actions that are natural and necessary to dog behavior, but may become intolerable if they appear when we don't think they should.

BARKING

Few things are more reassuring than knowing the dog will sound off when a stranger approaches the property.

Few things are more nerve-wracking than the incessant barking of a dog.

Therein lies the dilemma: We want the dog to bark, but *only* when we think it should.

Dogs bark for two reasons:

1. in response to some stimulus
2. for no apparent reason at all.

To bark or not to bark?

Barking in response to a stimulus

Wags is outside in the yard and some people walk by, so he barks. Once they have passed, he is quiet again. People passing are the stimulus that causes barking and once it has been removed, your dog stops.

If the people had stopped by the fence for a conversation, your dog would have continued to bark. To get Wags to stop, you have to

Changing Zeke's environment stopped his barking.

remove your dog or the people have to leave. If you live in a busy area, you may have to change your dog's environment.

Beverly would leave her Australian Shepherd, Zeke, in her apartment while she went to work. Zeke spent most of his day rushing from window to window barking wildly at all the activity outside. When Beverly confined him to the bedroom, with the shades drawn, he stayed calm and stopped barking.

Lesson: Remove the stimulus from the dog or the dog from the stimulus.

Your dog will also bark when he is in the house and someone comes to the door. After he has alerted you, tell your dog "thank you, that's enough" and, using the training you have learned in chapter 7, have him sit at your side as you answer the door. If necessary, use a leash so you can control him.

He may also rush to the window, stand there and bark because he sees or hears something. Again, thank him for letting you know what's going on and say "that's enough." If he does not stop, take him away from the window and have him lie down in a corner.

What happens if Wags does not want to stay in his corner? Review the "go lie down" you taught in chapter 8 to make sure he truly understands what it is you want and how important this exercise is to you.

Tell your dog "thank you" and then have him lie down.

Barking for no apparent reason

Your dog has a reason for barking but it may not be apparent to you. Frequently it is anxiety, boredom, loneliness or stress. None of these are difficult to overcome, if you work to eliminate these potential causes. Spend more time exercising your dog. Spend more time training your dog. Don't leave your dog alone so long or so often, etc.

If Wags still barks, you will need outside help. (See chapter 11.)

Barking in the crate

Again, your dog may be anxious, bored, lonely or stressed, in which case you have to spend more time with him.

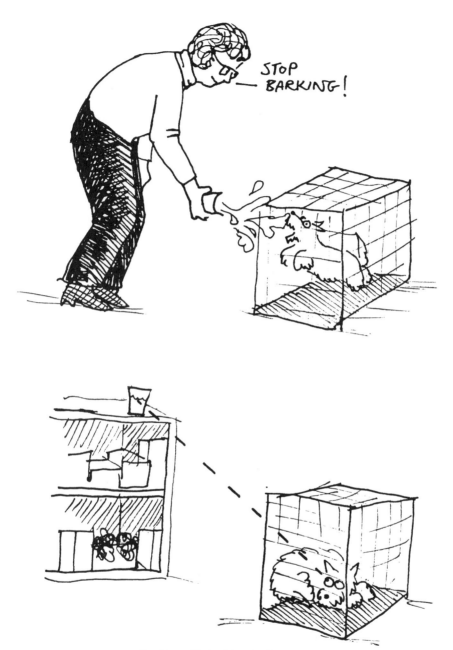

Dealing with barking in the crate.

He may also want out of the crate because you have left him in there too long or because he has to relieve himself.

Once you have eliminated these causes and your dog still barks, even though he has only been in the crate for a few minutes, you then must do something.

Use the water treatment to stop Wags's barking. Say "quiet" and toss one quarter of a paper cup of water toward his face. Refill the paper cup and put it on top of the crate or nearby so he can see it. After some repetition, your dog will be quiet just at the sight of the paper cup.

Once quiet for thirty seconds, let Wags out and tell him what a good boy he is. You must wait until he has been quiet for a while. If you let him out while barking, he learns that to get out of the crate all he has to do is bark.

Gradually increase the length of time in the crate before you let him out.

CHEWING

During teething, about four to six months of age, depending on the breed, Wags *must* chew. He cannot help it.

To get through this period, provide your dog with plenty of chew toys, both hard and soft, such as a Nylabone and a canvas field dummy. Stay away from toys your dog can destroy or ingest (rawhide). Food items, such as carrots or apples, dog biscuits or ice cubes, are great to relieve the monotony.

Make sure your dog does not have access to personal articles, such as shoes, socks, towels and so on. Do not give Wags an old sock of yours as a toy—he can't tell the difference between it and a new pair. Think of it as good training not to leave things lying around.

Chewing after a dog has gone through teething is usually a manifestation of anxiety, boredom, loneliness or stress. It is an oral habit that has nothing to do with being spiteful. Should Wags attack the furniture, baseboards and walls, tip over the garbage can or engage in other destructive chewing activities, use a crate when you can't supervise him. It will save you lots of money, not to mention losing your temper and getting mad at the poor fellow.

Use the same program for dealing with the causes of destructive chewing as you would for excessive barking: Spend more time exercising your dog. Spend more time training your dog. Don't leave your

Confinement

Suitable toys

Exercise

Dealing with chewing.

dog alone so long or so often, etc. A trained dog is a happy dog and a tired one is even happier!

In some cases, a dog may go to the extreme of self-mutilation because there is no other way for him to relieve tension. It rarely happens with a dog that is on a regular schedule with plenty of time with the family and that is properly exercised and trained.

DIGGING

Dogs like to dig for many reasons: to bury a bone, to dig up a bone, to see what's there, to look for cooler ground, to imitate the owner's gardening efforts, because it's fun, it's available, it relieves boredom, and on and on. Unspayed females, for example, may start digging twice a year to make a nest.

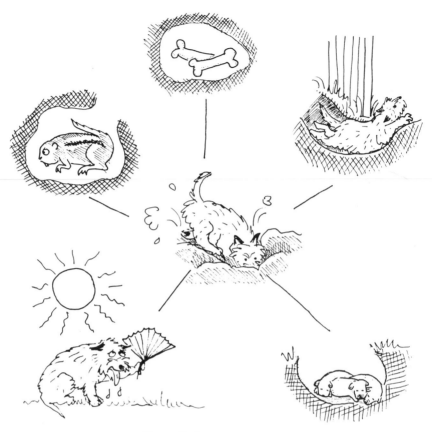

Dogs dig for many reasons.

Set aside an area where your dog can dig to his heart's content.

In some breeds, digging is more instinctive than in others. Terriers of all types are notorious and if you have one and don't want your garden rearranged, keep an eye on yours while he is out there. And that is the best prevention for digging—keeping an eye on your dog.

If you can't do that, set aside an area in the yard, such as a pen, where he can dig to his heart's content. Again, as with all behavior that could stem from boredom and frustration, examine how much time you are spending with your pet.

SUMMARY

1. If your dog barks in response to a stimulus, remove the stimulus or the dog.
2. If your dog barks for no apparent reason, spend more time with him.
3. For destructive chewing, give your dog more exercise and use your crate.
4. Dogs dig for many reasons, and with some breeds the behavior is highly instinctive.
5. If you can't set aside an area for your dog to dig, the best prevention is to keep an eye on him.
6. Remember—good behavior requires good exercise, good company, good health, good nutrition and good training.

Training strengthens the bond between man and dog.

Epilogue

USING THE APPROACH TO TRAINING described in this book, we have found that most dogs are quite content to go along with the program. More than that, they enjoy it and look forward to their regular sessions.

If you believe your dog will not love you anymore when you train for obedience, you are in for a surprise. Quite the opposite is the case, and training will make your dog more affectionate toward you. Through training comes respect, and through respect comes love.

With training you give your pet a job that makes the dog feel needed and wanted, which is important for mental well-being. You also give your dog some exercise, important for physical well-being.

When you experience what you perceive to be a problem, ask yourself "What is *my* responsibility toward its solution?" We start with the basic premise that it is rarely the dog's fault. If you truly do the same, the solution will come to you. On the other hand, if you always blame your dog, your relationship is doomed to failure.

Dogs demonstrate daily they are man's best friend. Now it is your turn to demonstrate you deserve that friend.

Bibliography

Bergman, Goran. *Why Does Your Dog Do That?* New York: Howell Book House, 1973.

Campbell, William E. *Behavior Problems in Dogs.* N.p.: American Veterinary Publications, 1975.

Evans, Job Michael. *The Evans Guide for Civilized City Canines.* New York: Howell Book House, 1989.

Lorenz, Konrad. *Man Meets Dog.* New York: Penguin Books, 1964.

Most, Konrad. *Training Dogs.* N.p.: Popular Dogs, 1954.

Pfaffenberger, Clarence J. *The New Knowledge of Dog Behavior.* New York: Howell Book House, 1963.

Pryor, Karen. *Don't Shoot the Dog!* New York: Simon & Schuster, 1984.

Volhard, Joachim J., and Gail T. Fisher. *Training Your Dog: The Step-by-Step Manual.* New York: Howell Book House, 1983.

Volhard, Joachim J., and Gail T. Fisher. *Teaching Dog Obedience Classes: The Manual for Instructors.* New York: Howell Book House, 1986.